Word Family File-Folder
Word Walls

by Mary Beth Spann

30 Reproducible Patterns for Portable Word Walls to Teach the Top Word Families and Help Kids Become Better Readers, Writers, and Spellers

SCHOLASTIC
PROFESSIONAL BOOKS

New York ☀ Toronto ☀ London ☀ Auckland ☀ Sydney
Mexico ☀ New Delhi ☀ Hong Kong ☀ Buenos Aires

Dedication

With lots of affection to Scholastic editor, Liza Charlesworth, who is happily expanding her family. And, with lots of love to my own family: Frank, Francesca and James.

Acknowledgments

Enormous thanks, as always, to Terry Cooper and Liza Charlesworth for your support and friendship, and for always understanding what teachers want and need so they may do their best for the children they serve. Thanks also to Josué Castilleja for his darling cover design, to the talented Jaime Lucero for his wonderful interior design, to artist Rusty Fletcher for his charming file-folder illustrations, and to editor Rebecca Callan for the caring and professional touch you brought to the project.

Cover design by Josué Castilleja
Illustrations by Rusty Fletcher
Interior design by Grafica, Inc.
ISBN: 0-439-26170-8

Contents

Contents

Introduction

Welcome to Word Family File-Folder Word Walls! This book contains adorable patterns and easy directions for creating 30 word family file-folder word walls which, when assembled, will each stand up on their own like greeting cards. The shapes are perfect for collecting and displaying words with various word family endings. All you need to do is duplicate each shape on a copying machine, mount it on the front of a file folder, then trim the top along the dash lines. The inside of each file folder is then ready for you to record a word bank of word family inspired words, while the back cover of each folder can be used to feature story-starter suggestions—either those provided in the book or ideas you dream up on your own!

The beauty of these word walls is that they are portable—they can be displayed on tabletops, transported to and from desks and learning centers, or popped into a self-sealing bag for take-home writing projects. With consistent use, you'll discover your file-folder word walls help improve students' awareness of word ending spelling patterns, spelling skills and vocabulary development, while adding intrigue and interest to the writing process. The word walls are easy to make and fun to use, so begin making your collection of Word Family File-Folder Word Walls today!

Super-Easy Word Wall How-To's

1. Duplicate the desired shape, plus story starters, on a copying machine. For an attractive, sturdy cover, consider copying or tracing the shape directly onto colored construction paper, oaktag, or craft foam that best matches the theme and design of the word wall (e.g., blue for the -ale whale shape, pink for the -ank piggy-bank pig shape, etc.). Use the Cover Decorating Tips offered with each word wall model to help guide your choices.

2. Use craft glue or rubber cement to mount the shape onto the front of a file folder, being careful to align edges labeled "Fold Edge" with corresponding folder edge. Use scissors to trim shape along dash lines.

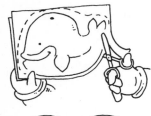

3. Open folder and use this space to copy the word wall title; the rest of the space will be used to record words featuring that word family ending.

4. Copy and cut out the "Story Starters" that accompany each file folder model. Glue each set of prompts to the back of the appropriate file-folder word wall.

5. Color and decorate shapes and labels. Look for specific Cover Decorating Tips offered with each word wall template. (**TIP:** Use permanent fine-line markers or a spray-on fixative to prevent smudging. Hair spray works well as an inexpensive fixative.)

Cover-Decorating Tips

Ready to decorate? Turn to the decorating tips that accompany each cover template in this book. Each tip helps you add texture, sparkle, and shine to your word family file folders! Short on time? Parents unable to volunteer in the classroom may be eager to construct word wall folder covers complete with special decorative touches.

Introducing Students to
File-Folder Word Walls

1. Prepare and share one or more of the portable word walls with your class. If you display a traditional word wall, point out how the file-folder word walls are portable mini-versions of your full-size word wall.

2. Note the folder cover details together. Help children realize that the name of each folder shape ends with that folder's word family ending.

3. Open the folder and show how the word wall title appears again on the inside cover.

4. Tell the children that you will use the blank space inside to collect words ending with that word family ending.

5. Use a fresh piece of chart pad paper to model how to write a story using some of the words recorded in the file-folder word wall. During this process, invite student input. "Think out loud" as you formulate what you are going to write. In this way, children can observe how you refer to the words both for inspiration and correct spellings.

Great Ideas for Collecting Word-Wall Words

☼ Offer children the suggested word list that accompanies each file-folder word wall model.

☼ Have children brainstorm words ending with the target word family sound and spelling pattern. Record children's suggestions on a large piece of chart pad paper. Then, as the class looks on, transfer these to the inside of the word wall's cover. Invite volunteers to insert small drawings next to words they wish to illustrate.

☼ When a child's first or last name contains one of the word family endings, include that child's name and school photo in the appropriate word family folder.

☼ Help children notice environmental print in the classroom, then record each word in its appropriate folder. Make a habit of collecting such words.

☼ Look through magazines and flyers to discover print logos; cut them out, glue each into its appropriate folder, then print the word(s) beneath each one.

☼ Lift words from literature. Aim to include favorite words, funny words, and frequently used words.

☼ Record spelling words.

☼ Include thematic words from cross-curricular studies.

☼ Look at the list of words that accompanies each file-folder model in this book. Present children with clues for each word. (For example, you might say "Our next word ends in -ack and means the opposite of front. That's right! It's the word *back*.") As children guess each word, record the words on the chart pad paper. Then, as the class looks on, transfer these to the inside of that word wall's folder. Use a dictionary to offer children clues to additional words you can include in each folder.

Putting File-Folder Word Walls to Work in Your Classroom

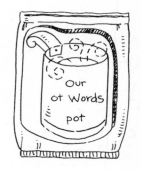

☼ Consider crafting your collection of file-folder word walls to coincide with the way you introduce word families in class. For example, if you introduce one word family per week, you can craft a new word family folder for use each week. If you introduce different word families to small groups of children or to individual students (depending on skill level and need), you can craft all of the folder shapes at once so they will be ready to go when you need them.

☼ Display individual folders along the edge of a chalk tray, in a front-facing bookcase or from an art-drying rack so children can easily identify and access them.

☼ Walk children through any management procedures you decide on, such as how to access, handle, and store the file-folder word walls.

☼ Demonstrate to children how they can refer to their file-folder word walls when searching for words to use in their writing. (**TIP:** Let children know that their word family file-folder word walls are particularly useful when they are searching for rhyming words to use when writing poetry and prose.)

Book Links

Looking for books that feature the word-family endings your students are studying? Turn to the Book Links that accompany each cover template in this book. Short on time? Parents unable to help in your classroom may volunteer to visit the local library. Or, ask your students to share their favorite word family books from home.

☀ Store portable word walls in an inexpensive cardboard or plastic file-folder box with a handle, thus making your collection truly portable. Place this box in your writing center. Students may then borrow word walls from the center and use them at their desks. Individual word walls may also be tacked to a bulletin board, propped up on a chalk tray, displayed on a tabletop easel, or clipped to a clothesline strung across the room. (**TIP:** Try making multiple copies of each word family file-folder word wall so more than one child at a time can work with the same words.)

☀ Build in ways for children to share their word wall-inspired writings (e.g., aloud, on a bulletin board display, in a class publication, etc.).

The 30 Word Family File-Folder Word Walls

well

Our -ell Words

snail

Our -ail Words

Our -at Words

cat

Our -ack Words

Let children pack this sack with lots of words that end in -ack!

Cover Decorating Tip

▶ Cut sack shape from brown or tan felt or craft foam. Use a black fineline marker to outline sack and to add details. Glue on a yarn drawstring and tie in a bow. Glue yarn ends in place. Glue sack shape to file-folder front.

Story Starters

▶ Cut and paste the following writing prompts onto the back of the file folder:

Our *-ack* Story Starters

☀ Write a rhyming poem telling about five things you can **crack**.

☀ Tell about how you might do some things differently if you could turn **back** time.

Book Links

• *Angus and the Ducks* by Marjorie Flack (Sunburst, 1997)

• *Five Little Ducks* (Raffi Songs to Read) by Raffi (Crown, 1992)

folder opens here

sack

Our -ack
Words

Our *-ail* Words

This little snail can leave a trail of words that end in -ail.

Cover Decorating Tip

▶ Cut snail shape from pink oaktag and glue to file-folder front. Outline details using a gray marker, gray puff paint, or silver glitter glue. Glue on googlie eyes.

Story Starters

▶ Cut and paste the following writing prompts onto the back of the file folder:

Our *-ail* Story Starters

☼ Tell about some **mail** you enjoyed receiving. Who sent it to you? Tell how it made you feel and why.

Book Links

• *The Puddle Pail* by Elisa Kleven (Dutton, 1997)

• *Walter's Tail* by Lisa Campbell Ernst (Aladdin Books, 1997)

snail

folder opens here

Our -ail Words

Our -*ain* Words

Suggested Word List

- **brain**
- **chain**
- **drain**
- **grain**
- **main**
- **pain**
- **plain**
- **rain**
- **Spain**
- **sprain**
- **stain**
- **train**
- **vain**

Book Links

• *Rain* by Peter Spier (Picture Yearling, 1997)

• *Train Song* by Harriet Ziefert (Orchard Books, 2000)

Climb aboard this special train and speed toward words that end in -ain.

Cover Decorating Tip

▶ Cut train shape from light-gray oaktag and glue to file-folder front. Outline train using a red marker, red puff paint, or silver glitter glue. Cut train wheels from extra pieces of gray oaktag. Use black marker to outline wheel details. Use brass fasteners to attach the center of each wheel to train so that wheels can turn. Glue a wisp of cotton batting to the train smokestack. Use a black crayon to shade the cotton so it resembles gray smoke.

Story Starters

▶ Cut and paste the following writing prompts onto the back of the file folder:

Our -*ain* Story Starters

☼ Tell about a real or pretend trip you took on a **train**. Who were you with? Where did you go? Tell about the trip's sights and sounds. What did you do to keep busy on your train trip?

train

Our -ain
Words

folder opens here

Our -*ake* Words

Our -ake Words

Suggested Word List

- bake
- brake
- cake
- drake
- fake
- flake
- Jake
- lake
- make
- quake
- rake
- sake
- shake
- snowflake
- stake
- take
- wake

Book Links

• *Pancakes, Pancakes!* by Eric Carle (Aladdin Paperbacks, 1998)

• *Shake My Sillies Out* (Raffi Songs to Read) by Raffi (Crown, 1990)

This sparkling snowflake will help you make lots of words that end in -ake.

Cover Decorating Tip

▶ Cut snowflake shape from white oaktag or craft foam and glue to file-folder front. Outline snowflake using silver glitter glue. Add more details using pale blue puff paints.

Story Starters

▶ Cut and paste the following writing prompts onto the back of the file folder:

Our -*ake* Story Starters

☼ Write the recipe and directions for how to **bake** your favorite **cake**. Or, describe a cake someone made for you.

☼ List all the things you do when you **wake** up on a school morning. Then, **make** a separate list of all the things you do when you wake up on a day there is no school.

Our -ake Words

folder opens here

Our *-ale* Words

Suggested Word List

bale
Dale
gale
kale
male
pale
sale
scale
stale
tale
whale

Book Links

• *Big Blue Whale* by Nicola Davies (Candlewick Press, 1997)

• *Caps for Sale: A Tale of a Peddler, Some Monkeys and Their Monkey Business* by Esphyr Slobodkina (HarperTrophy, 1996)

Let this whale help tell tales using words that end in -ale.

Cover Decorating Tip

▶ Cut whale shape from blue and white oaktag or craft foam and glue to file-folder front. Use black fineline marker to outline whale and to trace over whale details. Glue on googlie eyes.

Story Starters

▶ Cut and paste the following writing prompts onto the back of the file folder:

Our *-ale* Story Starters

☼ Retell a favorite **tale** you love hearing again and again.

☼ Tell about a time you were able to buy something because it was on **sale**.

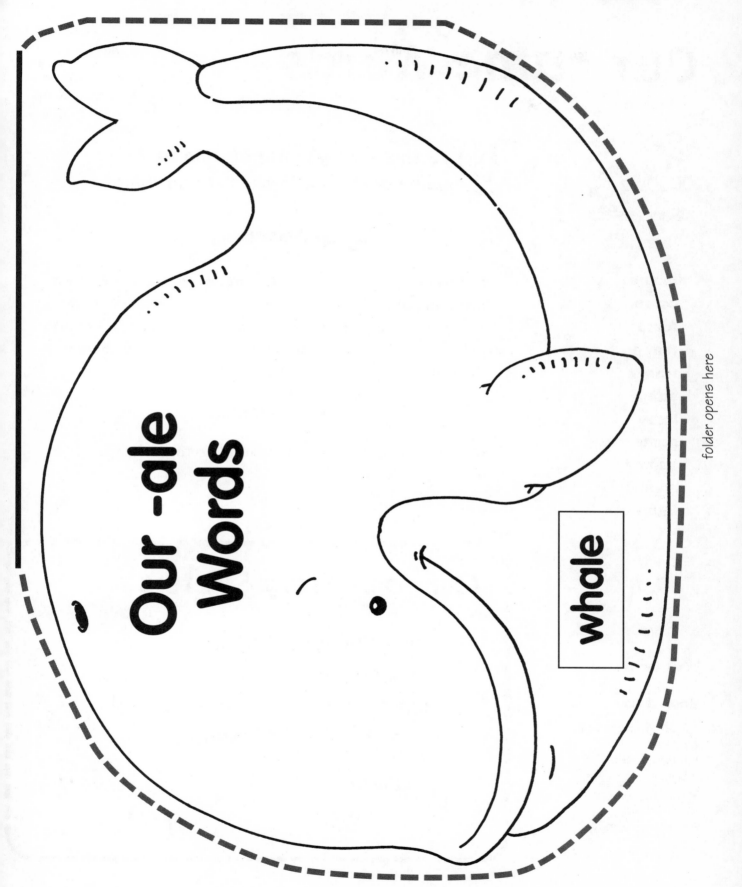

Our -ale
Words

whale

folder opens here

Our -*ame* Words

Our -ame
Words

frame

Suggested Word List

blame
came
fame
flame
frame
game
lame
name
same
shame
tame

Use this pretty picture frame to name some words that end in -ame.

Cover Decorating Tip

▶ Cut frame shape from light-brown or tan oaktag or craft foam and glue to file-folder front. Outline frame and add details using a black marker. Use a gold gelpen, gold nail polish, or gold craft paint to add "gilded" touches to inside the frame's decorative scrolls.

Story Starters

▶ Cut and paste the following writing prompts onto the back of the file folder:

Our -*ame* Story Starters

☼ List all the **names** of every family member you can think of. Pick two names off your list and tell how all three of you are the **same**.

Matthew   Chris   Beth

Sara   Mark

Book Links

• *A My Name Is Alice* by Jane Bayer (Dutton, 1992)

• *Mommy Doesn't Know My Name* by Suzanne Williams (Houghton Mifflin, 1996)

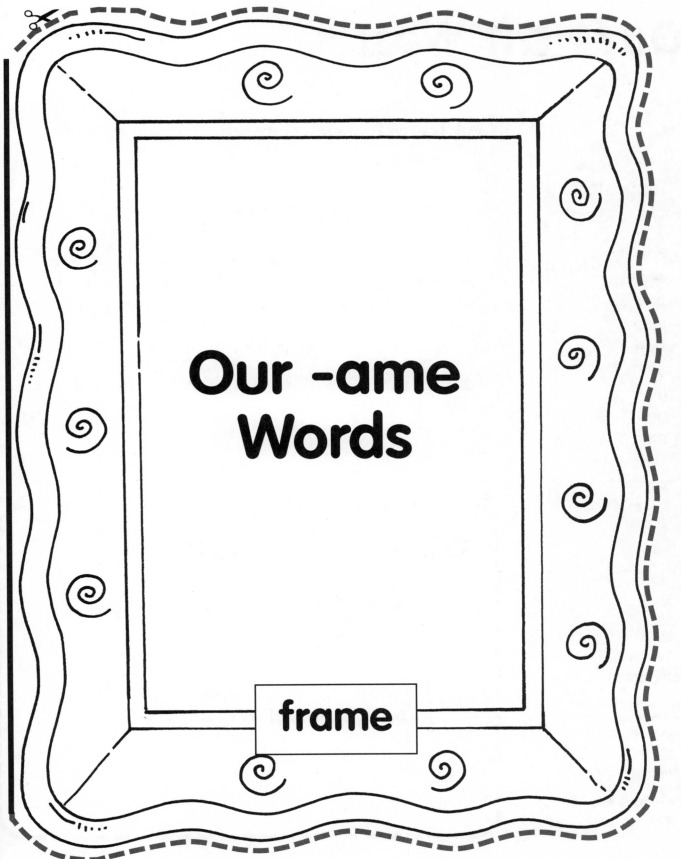

**Our -ame
Words**

frame

folder opens here

Our -*an* Words

Suggested Word List

ban
bran
can
clan
Dan
fan
man
pan
plan
ran
scan
span
tan
than
van

Plan to use this fan for words ending in -an.

Cover Decorating Tip

▶ Cut fan shape from any pastel-color oaktag or craft foam and glue to file-folder front. Use fineline markers to outline and add details. Then, glue lace to the top edge of fan.

Story Starters

▶ Cut and paste the following writing prompts onto the back of the file folder:

Our -*an* Story Starters

☼ Make a list of things you know you **can** do well.

☼ Tell how you would **plan** a surprise party for a friend or family member.

Book Links

• *The Gingerbread Man* by Eric Kimmel (Holiday House, 1993)

• *The Magic Fan* by Keith Baker (Harcourt Brace, 1989)

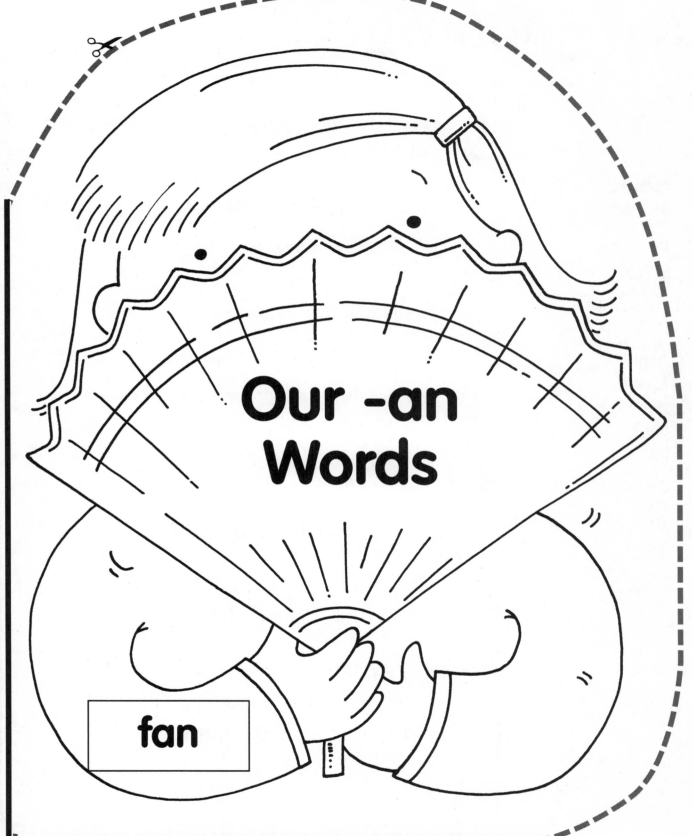

Our -an
Words

folder opens here

fan

Our -ank Words

Our -ank
Words

Suggested Word List

bank

blank

clank

crank

drank

flank

Frank

Hank

lank

plank

prank

rank

sank

tank

thank

yank

Book Links

• *Charlotte's Piggy Bank* by David McKee (Andersen Press, 1996)

• *Richard Scarry's Please and Thank You Book* by Richard Scarry (Random House, 1973)

Deposit words ending in -ank into this cute little piggy bank.

Cover Decorating Tip

▶ Cut piggy-bank shape from pink oaktag or craft foam and glue to file-folder front. Use a black marker to outline the bank shape and to add details. Color bank's coin slot black. Glue on play coins and googlie eyes.

Story Starters

▶ Cut and paste the following writing prompts onto the back of the file folder:

Our *-ank* Story Starters

☼ Tell what you would do if you had a million dollars in the **bank**.

☼ Write a fictitious story telling about a time you **drank** a magic potion that made your mind go **blank**.

Our -ank
Words

bank

folder opens here

Our -ap Words

Our -ap Words

Suggested Word List

- cap
- chap
- clap
- flap
- gap
- lap
- map
- nap
- tap
- sap
- scrap
- strap
- tap
- trap
- wrap
- yap

With this cap you can bat home-run words that end in -ap.

Cover Decorating Tip

▶ Cut cap shape from light-blue oaktag or craft foam and glue to file-folder front. Use a green marker to color in details.

Story Starters

▶ Cut and paste the following writing prompts onto the back of the file folder:

Our -ap Story Starters

☀ Draw and label a **map** of your classroom or bedroom.

☀ Make a list of ten items that have a **strap**.

Book Links

• *Caps for Sale: A Tale of a Peddler, Some Monkeys and Their Monkey Business* by Esphyr Slobodkina (HarperTrophy, 1996)

• *Me on the Map* by Joan Sweeney (Dragonfly, 1998)

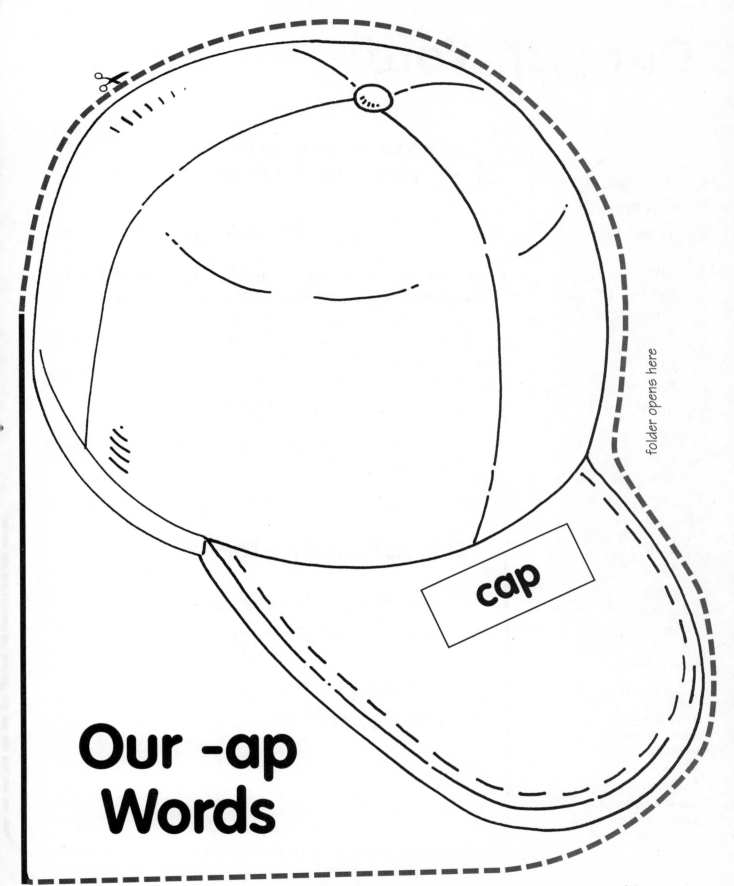

folder opens here

cap

Our -ap Words

Our -at Words

Suggested Word List

- bat
- brat
- cat
- chat
- fat
- flat
- gnat
- hat
- mat
- pat
- rat
- sat
- scat
- slat
- spat
- that

Book Links

- *The Cat in the Hat* by Dr. Seuss (Random House, 1957)

- *The Fat Cat Sat on the Mat* by Nurit Karlin (HarperCollins Junior, 1996)

This little cat loves to bat at all the words that end in -at.

Cover Decorating Tip

▶ Cut cat shape from tan oaktag or craft foam and glue to file-folder front. Glue on a pink nose cut from oaktag or craft foam. Use fineline markers to outline cat and add cat details. Glue on broom-straw whiskers, googlie eyes, and a real ribbon bow tie.

Story Starters

▶ Cut and paste the following writing prompts onto the back of the file folder:

Our *-at* Story Starters

- ☼ Tell what you need to do to take care of a pet **cat**.

- ☼ Tell why you do or do not like to **chat** on the phone.

Our -at
Words

cat

folder opens here

Our -ate Words

Open up this garden gate to welcome words that end in -ate.

Suggested Word List

crate

date

fate

gate

grate

Kate

late

mate

plate

rate

skate

slate

state

Cover Decorating Tip

▶ Cut gate shape from white oaktag or craft foam and glue to file-folder front. Use fineline markers to outline gate, to add details, and to color in leaves and flowers. Or, use a glue gun (adult use only) to glue on artificial leaves and flowers.

Story Starters

▶ Cut and paste the following writing prompts onto the back of the file folder:

Our -ate Story Starters

☼ Tell about a time you were **late**. Why were you late? How did being late make you feel? How can you make sure you won't be late again?

Book Links

• *My Sister Ate One Hare* by Bill Grossman (Random House, 1998)

• *Slip, Slide, Skate!* by Gail Herman (Scholastic, 2000)

fold edge

folder opens here

Our -ate Words

gate

Our -ay Words

Our -ay Words

jay

Suggested Word List

bay
clay
day
gray
hay
lay
jay
lay
May
pay
play
ray
say
spay
stay
stray
sway

Book Links

• *Happy Birthday, Davy!* by Brigitte Weninger (North South Books, 2000)

• *100th Day Worries* by Margery Cuyler (Simon & Schuster, 2000)

This little jay wants to say there are lots of words that end with -ay.

Cover Decorating Tip

▷ Cut shape from white oaktag or craft foam and glue to file folder front. Use black fineline marker to outline the jay shape and a blue marker to fill in the bird's markings. Glue on googlie eyes and a few blue craft feathers. Then, color the leaves green and branches brown.

Story Starters

▷ Cut and paste the following writing prompts onto the back of the file folder:

Our -ay Story Starters

☼ Tell about the best **day** you ever had, then tell about the worst day you ever had.

☼ Describe your perfect **day**. Where would you go? What would you do? Who would you spend your perfect day with?

Our -ay Words

jay

folder opens here

Our -eat Words

Suggested Word List

- beat
- bleat
- cheat
- cleat
- feat
- heat
- meat
- neat
- peat
- pleat
- seat
- treat
- wheat

Harvest words that end in -eat and store them in this bundle of wheat.

Cover Decorating Tip

▶ Cut wheat shape from tan oaktag or craft foam and glue to file-folder front. Use black or brown fineline marker to outline wheat and to add wheat details.

Story Starters

▶ Cut and paste the following writing prompts onto the back of the file folder:

Our -eat Story Starters

☺ Make a list of foods you like to **eat** for a **treat**.

☺ Tell what it means to **cheat**. Explain why people might cheat. Tell if you think it is ever okay to cheat.

Book Links

- *Eat Your Peas* by Kes Gray (DK Publishing, 2000)

- *Little Miss Neat* by Robert Hargreaves (Price Stern Sloan, 1998)

**Our -eat
Words**

wheat

folder opens here

Our -*ell* Words

Suggested Word List

- bell
- cell
- dell
- dwell
- fell
- jell
- Nell
- sell
- shell
- smell
- spell
- swell
- tell
- well
- yell

Book Links

• *The Doorbell Rang* by Pat Hutchins (Greenwillow, 1986)

• *The Farmer in the Dell* by John O'Brien (Boyds Mills Press, 2000)

Words ending in -ell can easily dwell deep inside this wishing well.

Cover Decorating Tip

▶ Cut well shape from gray or tan oaktag or craft foam and glue to file-folder front. Use black fineline marker to outline and to fill in well details. Dip the tip of a pencil eraser into white paint and use to dab a bit of "concrete-look" onto each brick shape.

Story Starters

▶ Cut and paste the following writing prompts onto the back of the file folder:

Our -*ell* Story Starters

☼ Make a list of things you love to **smell**.

☼ Make a list of things you think **smell** icky.

well

Our -ell
Words

folder opens here

Our -est Words

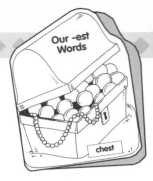

Suggested Word List

- best
- chest
- crest
- jest
- nest
- pest
- quest
- rest
- test
- vest
- west
- zest

Use this special treasure chest to stash your words that end in -est.

Cover Decorating Tip

▶ Cut chest shape from blue or brown oaktag or craft foam and glue to file-folder front. Use fineline markers to outline chest and to add details. Cut and glue circles of aluminum foil or gold-foil wrapping paper to serve as coins.

Story Starters

▶ Cut and paste the following writing prompts onto the back of the file folder:

Our -est Story Starters

- ☼ Tell how you feel when you have to take a **test**. Tell also how you get ready to take a test.

- ☼ Tell if you think it's possible to have more than one **best** friend.

Book Links

• *The Best Nest* by P. D. Eastman (Random House, 1968)

• *Henry and Mudge Take the Big Test: The Tenth Book of Their Adventures* by Cynthia Rylant (Simon & Schuster, 1997)

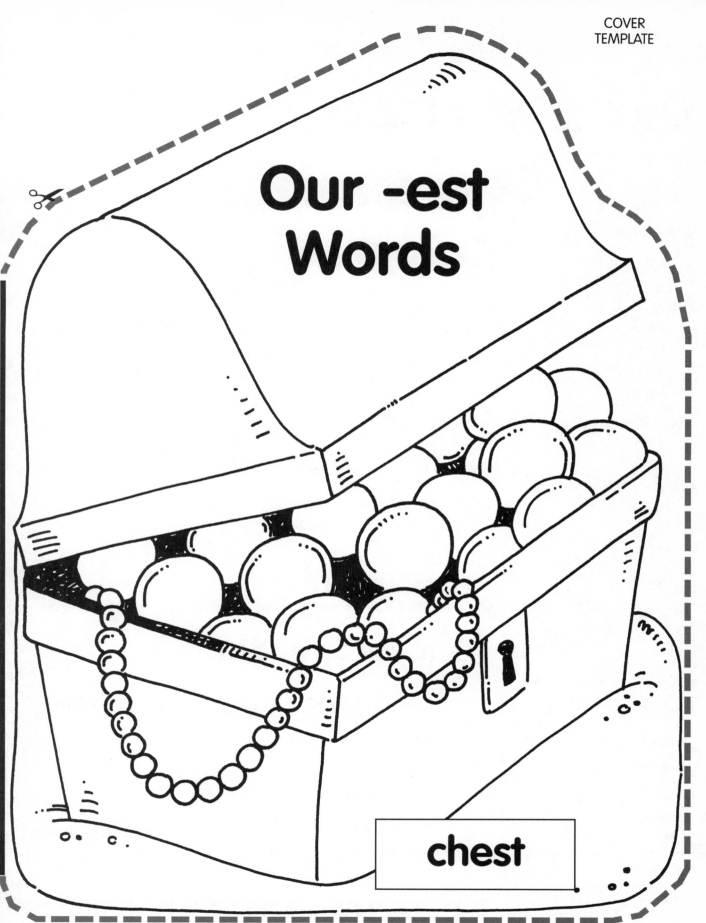

Our -est Words

chest

folder opens here

Our -ice Words

Suggested Word List

- dice
- lice
- mice
- nice
- price
- rice
- slice
- spice
- splice
- thrice
- twice
- vice

These nice little mice gather words that end in -ice.

Cover Decorating Tip

▶ Cut folder background shape from any pastel-color oaktag. Color and cut out cheese and mice from file folder pattern. Glue paper cheese and mice to background. Then, glue on tiny googlie eyes, broom-straw whiskers, and ribbon bow ties.

Story Starters

▶ Cut and paste the following writing prompts onto the back of the file folder:

Our -ice Story Starters

☀ Make a list of things you can get by the **slice**.

☀ Tell how to cook your favorite meal that is served with **rice**.

Book Links

• *Chicken Soup with Rice* by Maurice Sendak (Scholastic, 1992)

• *Mrs. Brice's Mice* by Syd Hoff (HarperCollins Children's Books, 1988)

mice

Our -ice
Words

folder opens here

Our -*ick* Words

Suggested Word List

brick

chick

click

flick

kick

lick

Nick

pick

quick

Rick

sick

slick

stick

thick

tick

trick

Book Links

• *The Chick and the Duckling* adapted by Mirra Gingsburg (Aladdin Paperbacks, 1988)

• *Monkey Monkey's Trick: Based on an African Folktale* by Patricia McKissack (Random House, 1988)

This little chick likes to pick at all the words that end with -ick.

Cover Decorating Tip

▶ Cut shape from light-blue oaktag or craft foam. Use black fineline marker to trace chick pattern onto yellow oaktag or craft foam; cut out and glue to file folder front. Use fineline markers to add chick details, to color beak and legs orange, and to draw on leaves and flowers. Glue on a googlie eye and a few yellow craft feathers.

Story Starters

▶ Cut and paste the following writing prompts onto the back of the file folder:

Our -*ick* Story Starters

☼ Tell what you do to help yourself feel better when you are **sick**.

☼ Tell about a magic **trick** you saw some-one perform.

chick

Our -ick Words

folder opens here

Our *-ide* Words

Suggested Word List

bride

glide

hide

inside

pride

ride

side

slide

snide

stride

tide

wide

Book Links

• *Life in a Tide Pool* by Allan Fowler (Children's Press, 1997)

• *Snow Inside the House* by Sean Diviny (HarperCollins, 1998)

Take a ride down this slide—it's filled with words that end in *-ide*.

Cover Decorating Tip

▶ Cut slide shape from gray oaktag and glue to file folder front. Color and cut out paper child from file folder pattern. Glue paper child to slide. Outline slide with glitter glue; let dry.

Story Starters

▶ Cut and paste the following writing prompts onto the back of the file folder:

Our *-ide* Story Starters

☀ Tell about a time you took a **ride** on a water **slide**. How did it make you feel **inside**?

☀ Tell about a time you took **pride** in something you did.

slide

Our -ide Words

folder opens here

Our *-ight* Words

All day and all night this knight guards words that end in -ight.

Suggested Word List

- blight
- bright
- Dwight
- fight
- flight
- fright
- knight
- light
- might
- night
- plight
- right
- sight
- slight
- tight

Book Links

- *Good Night, Gorilla* by Peggy Rathman (Puffin, 2000)
- *Goodnight, Moon* by Margaret Wise Brown (HarperFestival, 1991)

Cover Decorating Tip

▶ Cut folder shape from gray oaktag or craft foam and glue to file-folder front. Use fineline markers to outline knight and to add details. Outline details with silver glitter glue.

Story Starters

▶ Cut and paste the following writing prompts onto the back of the file folder:

Our *-ight* Story Starters

 Tell about a time you and someone you care about had a **fight** with words. How did the fight get started? How was it solved? How would you do things differently next time?

Our -ight
Words

knight

folder opens here

Our *-ill* Words

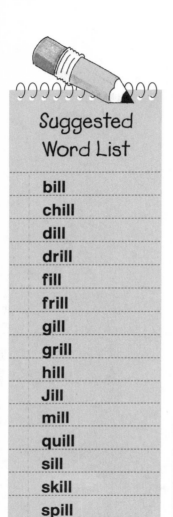

Suggested Word List

bill
chill
dill
drill
fill
frill
gill
grill
hill
Jill
mill
quill
sill
skill
spill
still
thrill

Book Links

• *The Magic Hill* by A.A. Milne (Dutton Books, 2000)

• *Pecos Bill: A Tall Tale* by Steven Kellogg (William Morrow, 1986)

On the other side of this big round hill are lots of words that end in -ill.

Cover Decorating Tip

▶ Cut hill shape from white oaktag and glue to file folder front. Color and cut out paper child from file folder pattern. Glue paper child to hill as shown. Brush hill with white glue and sprinkle with translucent "diamond dust" glitter.

Story Starters

▶ Cut and paste the following writing prompts onto the back of the file folder:

Our *-ill* Story Starters

☼ Tell about a time you felt **ill**. How did you feel when you were ill? Did you get a **chill**? What did you do to help yourself get better? Did you have to take a **pill**? How did you pass the time?

☼ Make up a story about a big **spill**.

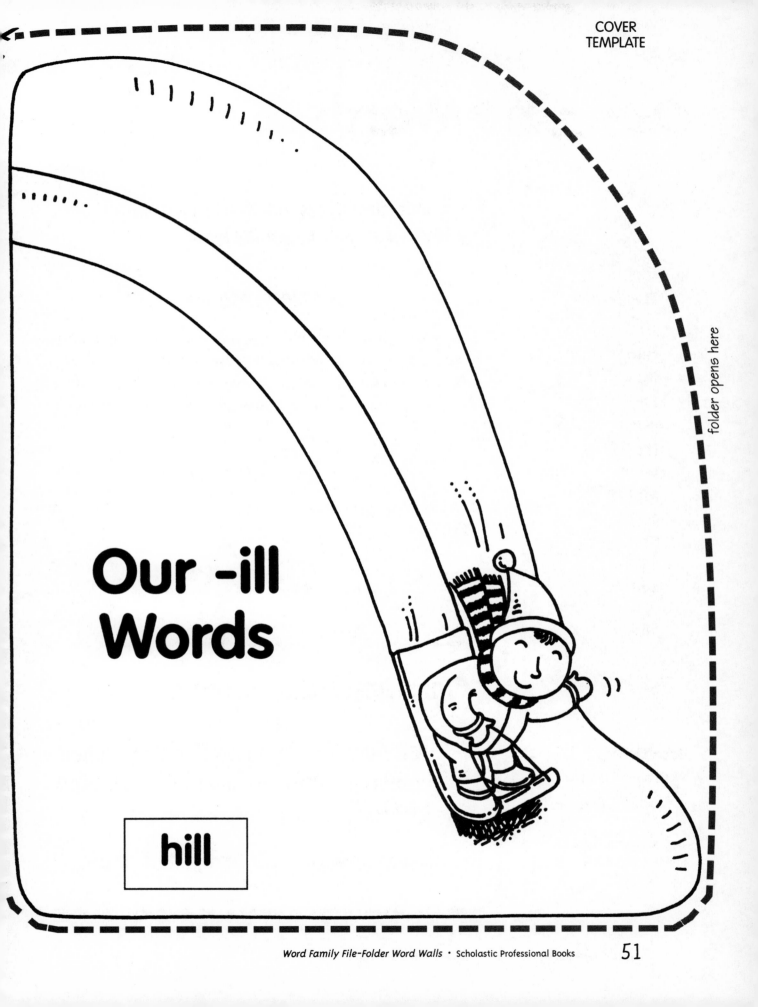

folder opens here

Our -ill Words

hill

Our -*ine* Words

Let this pretty ivy vine curl round your words that end in -ine.

Suggested Word List

dine

fine

line

mine

nine

pine

shine

shrine

spine

swine

tine

twine

vine

whine

Cover Decorating Tip

▶ Cut folder shape from white or light-blue oaktag or craft foam. Use a brown marker to draw on vine, and a green marker to draw on leaves. Or, use a glue gun (adult use only) to glue on brown rug yarn or hemp-like rope to resemble vine. Then, glue on artificial leaves.

Story Starters

▶ Cut and paste the following writing prompts onto the back of the file folder:

Our -*ine* Story Starters

☼ Tell about a time you tried to **whine** to get your way. Did it work? Why or why not?

☼ Make a list of **nine** things that **shine**.

Book Links

• *Big Pumpkin* by Erica Silverman (Aladdin Paperbacks, 1995)

• *It's Mine* by Leo Lionni (Dragonfly, 1996)

Our -ine Words

vine

folder opens here

Our -*ing* Words

This ring fit for a king will encircle your words that end in -ing.

Suggested Word List

bing
bring
cling
ding
fling
king
ping
ring
sing
sling
spring
sting
string
swing
thing
wing
wring

Book Links

• *Babar the King* by Jean De Brunhoff (Random House, 1963)

• *Poppleton in Spring* by Cynthia Rylant (Scholastic, 1999)

Cover Decorating Tip

▶ Cut ring shape from yellow oaktag or craft foam and glue to file-folder front. Use black fineline marker to trace over ring, and to add details, and to color in ring hole. Brush gem with white craft glue and sprinkle with silver glitter; let dry.

Story Starters

▶ Cut and paste the following writing prompts onto the back of the file folder:

Our -*ing* Story Starters

☼ Tell how you would rule if you were **king** of the school.

☼ Make up a story about finding a gold **ring** that can **sing**.

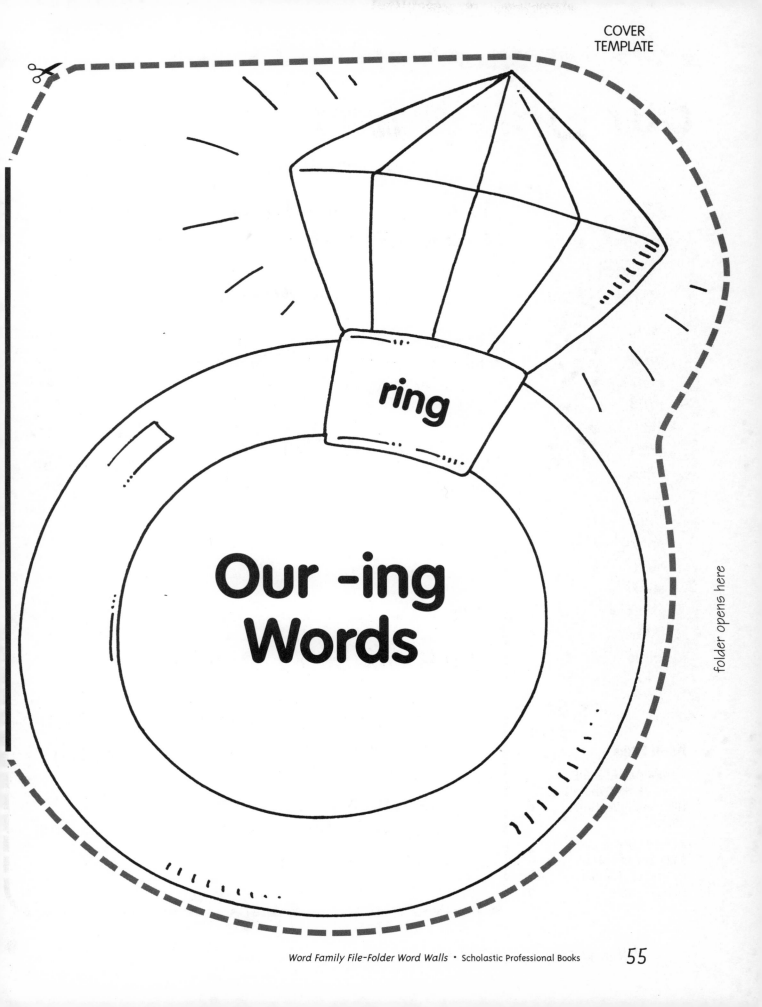

ring

Our -ing Words

folder opens here

Our *-ink* Words

Suggested Word List

- blink
- brink
- clink
- drink
- kink
- link
- mink
- pink
- rink
- shrink
- sink
- slink
- stink
- think
- wink

Book Links

• *Mike Swan, Sink or Swim* by Deborah Heiligman (Yearling, 1998)

• *Oh! The Things You Can Think!* by Dr. Seuss (Random House, 1989)

Just think! You'll fill this sink in a wink with many words that end in -ink.

Cover Decorating Tip

▶ Cut sink shape from white oaktag or craft foam and glue to file-folder front. Use fineline markers to trace over sink details. Use silver glitter glue to fill in sink faucet and handles.

Story Starters

▶ Cut and paste the following writing prompts onto the back of the file folder:

Our *-ink* Story Starters

☼ Write a story about a magical **pink drink** that makes you **shrink** when you drink it.

☼ Tell about your first time skating in an ice **rink** or a roller rink.

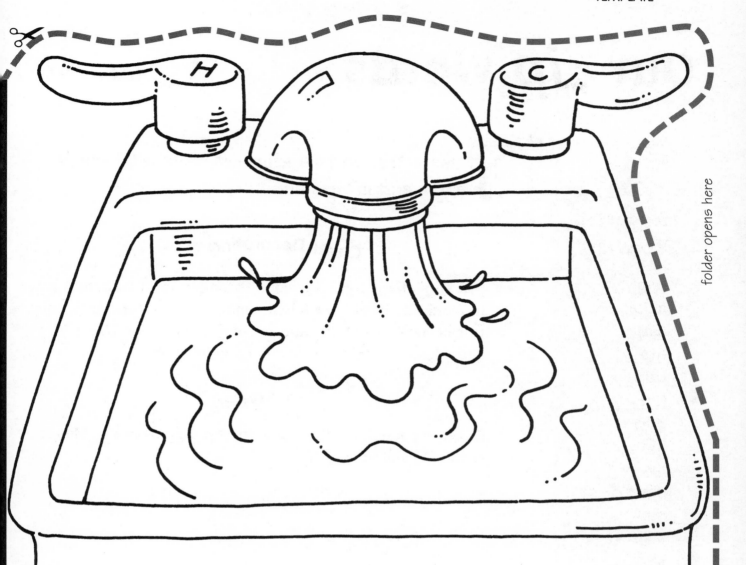

folder opens here

Our -ink
Words

sink

Our *-ip* Words

Suggested Word List

- blip
- chip
- clip
- dip
- drip
- flip
- grip
- hip
- lip
- nip
- rip
- ship
- sip
- skip
- slip
- snip
- strip

Book Links

- *Meg and Jim's Sled Trip* by Laura Appleton-Smith (Flyleaf, 1998)

- *On the Mayflower: Voyage of the Ship's Apprentice & a Passenger Girl* by Kate Waters (Scholastic, 1999)

Take a trip on this ship—it sails with words that end in -ip.

Cover Decorating Tip

▶ Cut ship shape from any color oaktag or craft foam and glue to file-folder front. Use fineline markers to outline ship, to trace over ship details, and to color in windows. Use gold glitter glue to highlight details on ship's body.

Story Starters

▶ Cut and paste the following writing prompts onto the back of the file folder:

Our *-ip* Story Starters

☼ Tell about a **trip** you'd love to take on a **ship**.

☼ Make up a poem about doing a **flip** after taking a **slip**.

ship

Our -ip Words

folder opens here

Our -ock Words

Stock this sock with words that end in -ock.

Our -ock Words

Suggested Word List

block
clock
crock
dock
flock
frock
knock
lock
mock
rock
shock
smock
sock
stock
tock

Cover Decorating Tip

▶ Cut sock shape from any color oaktag or self-sticking felt and adhere to file-folder front. Use fineline markers to outline and fill in sock details.

Story Starters

▶ Cut and paste the following writing prompts onto the back of the file folder:

Book Links

• *Everybody Needs a Rock* by Byrd Baylor (Atheneum, 1974)

• *I Am a Rock* by Jean Marzollo (Cartwheel Books, 1998)

Our -ock Story Starters

☼ Write a story about finding a magic **rock**.

☼ Tell about a time that you were so surprised you were in **shock**.

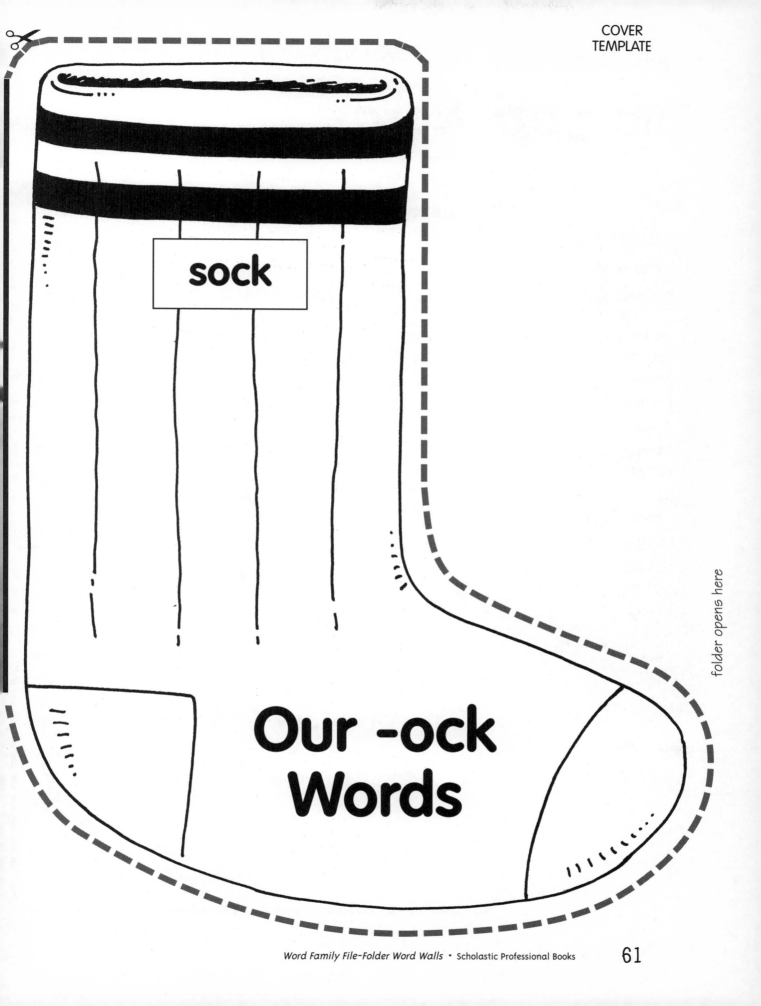

sock

Our -ock
Words

folder opens here

Our -op Words

This mop will sop up words that end in -op.

Suggested Word List

bop

chop

cop

crop

drop

flop

hop

mop

plop

pop

prop

shop

slop

sop

stop

top

Book Links

• *Hop on Pop* by Dr. Seuss (Random House, 1963)

• *Stop That Pickle*! by Peter Armour (Houghton Mifflin, 1993)

Cover Decorating Tip

▶ Cut mop shape from white oaktag or craft foam and glue to file-folder front. Use markers to outline and color in picture details. Glue scraps of white yarn to the mop top. Add blue glitter to water drops and puddle outline.

Story Starters

▶ Cut and paste the following writing prompts onto the back of the file folder:

Our -op Story Starters

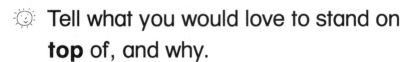

☼ Tell why you love or hate to **shop**.

☼ Tell what you would love to stand on **top** of, and why.

mop

Our -op Words

folder opens here

Our -ot Words

Our -ot Words

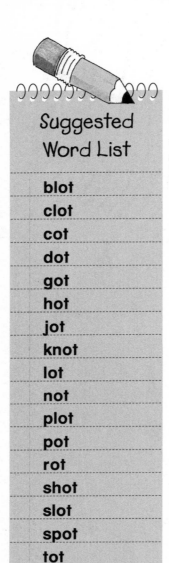

Book Links

• *Hot Dog* by Molly Coxe (Golden Books, 1999)

• *Ten Black Dots* by Donald Crews (Mulberry, 1995)

Fill this pot up to the top with lots of words that end in -ot.

Cover Decorating Tip

▶ Cut pot shape from gray oaktag or craft foam and glue to file-folder front. Use black fineline markers to outline pot and to fill in pot handle. Brush pot "shine" spot with a bit of white craft glue. Sprinkle with translucent "diamond dust" glitter; let dry.

Story Starters

▶ Cut and paste the following writing prompts onto the back of the file folder:

Our -ot Story Starters

☀ Tell whether you would rather be too **hot** or too cold.

☀ Make a list of things that have spots or **dots**.

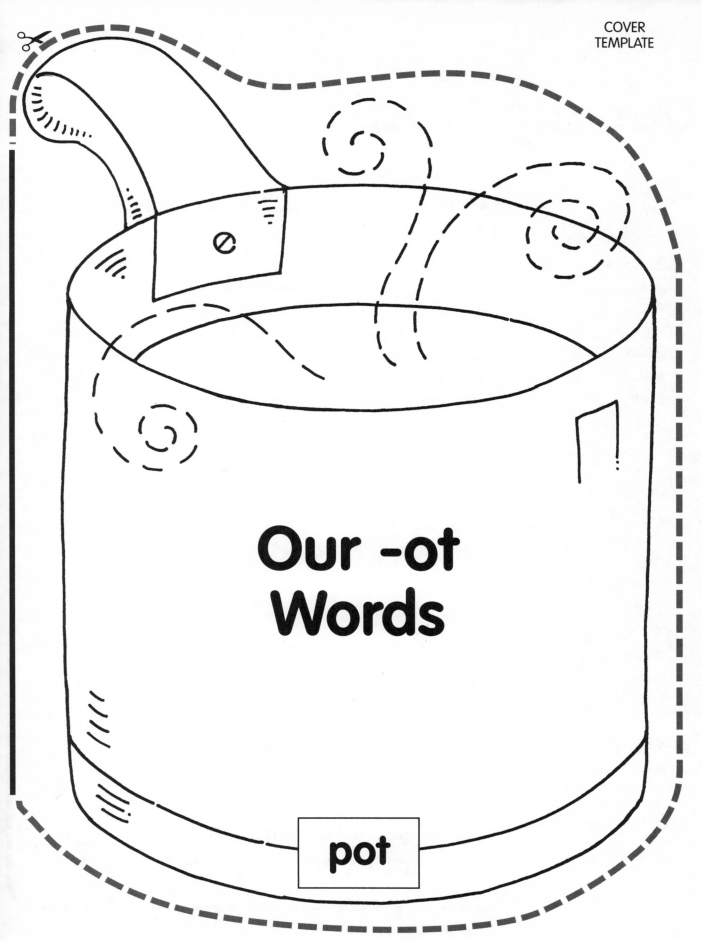

Our -ot
Words

pot

folder opens here

Our -ug Words

Suggested Word List

bug
chug
drug
dug
hug
jug
lug
mug
plug
pug
rug
shrug
slug
smug
snug
thug
tug

This funny, little doodle bug will hug all your words that end in -ug.

Cover Decorating Tip

▶ Cut folder shape from any color oaktag or craft foam. Use black fineline marker to outline bug shape, and red or green marker to color in bug details. Glue on googlie eyes. Brush spots with white craft glue. Sprinkle with translucent "diamond dust" glitter; let dry.

Story Starters

▶ Cut and paste the following writing prompts onto the back of the file folder:

Our -ug Story Starters

☼ Tell what you think this saying means: He's "**snug** as a **bug** in a **rug**."

☼ Make a list of **bugs** you might find near your home.

Book Links

• *The Grouchy Ladybug* by Eric Carle (HarperFestival, 1999)

• *Rug Bug* by Tennant Redbank (Golden Books, 2000)

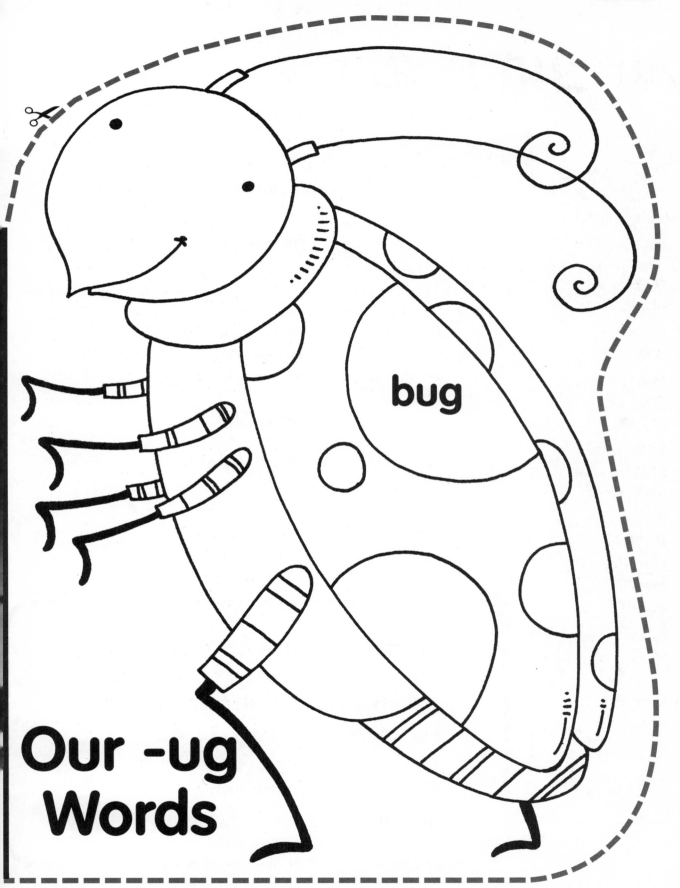

bug

Our -ug Words

folder opens here

Our -*ump* Words

Suggested Word List

- bump
- chump
- clump
- dump
- frump
- grump
- hump
- jump
- lump
- plump
- pump
- rump
- slump
- stump
- thump
- trump

Book Links

• *The Grump* by Mark Ludy (Green Pastures Publishing, 2000)

• *Jump, Frog, Jump!* by Robert Kalan (William Morrow & Co., 1995)

Peek inside this tree-trunk stump, then jot some words that end in -ump.

Cover Decorating Tip

▶ Cut stump shape from brown or tan oaktag or craft foam and glue directly to file folder. Use a black marker to outline stump and to add details. Use a green marker to color in grassy tufts. Brush a bit of white craft glue on the top of the stump. Sprinkle with translucent "diamond dust" glitter; let dry.

Story Starters

▶ Cut and paste the following writing prompts onto the back of the file folder:

Our -*ump* Story Starters

☼ Tell what you think this saying means: He sat like a "**bump** on a log."

☼ Tell what turns you into a **grump**.

Our -ump
Words

folder opens here

stump

Our -unk Words

This very spunky little skunk sniffs out words that end in -unk.

Suggested Word List

bunk
chunk
drunk
dunk
flunk
funk
hunk
junk
plunk
shrunk
skunk
slunk
spunk
stunk
sunk
trunk

Book Links

• *Katie's Trunk* by Ann Warren Turner (Aladdin Paperbacks, 1997)

• *Lizzy and Skunk* by Mary-Louise Fitzpatrick (DK Publishing, 2000)

Cover Decorating Tip

▶ Cut folder shape from white felt or craft foam. Use black fineline marker to outline skunk and a black wide-tipped marker to color in markings. Glue on a ribbon bow tie. Glue on googlie eyes.

Story Starters

▶ Cut and paste the following writing prompts onto the back of the file folder:

Our -unk Story Starters

☼ Make a list of all the foods you like to **dunk**—and what you like to dunk those foods into.

☼ Tell what you think this saying means: "One person's **junk** is another person's treasure."

Our -unk Words

skunk

folder opens here

notes